W9-BEG-780

_____

was confirmed by_____

at the parish of_____

on _____ in the year_____

and received this book from

_____

Do you believe in the holy catholic Church,
the communion of saints, the forgiveness
of sins,
the resurrection of the body,
and life everlasting?

This is our faith. This is the faith
of the Church.
We are proud to profess it in Christ Jesus
our Lord.

—*Rite of Confirmation, no. 23*

RESOURCES

Unless otherwise noted, excerpts from scripture are from the *New Revised Standard Version of the Bible* © 1989 Division of Christian Education of the National Council for the Churches of Christ in the United States of America. All rights reserved.

Scripture excerpts noted NAB are taken from the *New American Bible with Revised New Testament and Psalms* © 1991, 1986, 1970 Confraternity of Christian Doctrine, Inc., Washington, DC. Used with permission. All rights reserved. No part of the *New American Bible* may be reproduced by any means without permission in writing from the copyright owner.

Excerpts of the Psalms are from *The Psalms: Grail Translation from the Hebrew* © 1993 by Ladies of the Grail (England). Used by permission of GIA Publications, Inc., exclusive agent. All rights reserved.

The English translation of the prayers for the consecration of the chrism from the *Rite of Confirmation, Rite of the Blessing of Oils, Rite of Consecrating the Chrism* © 1972, International Committee on English in the Liturgy, Inc. (ICEL); excerpts from the English translation of Eucharistic Prayer III from *The Roman Missal* © 1973, ICEL; the English translation of the Prayer of the Penitent from the *Rite of Penance* © 1974, ICEL; excerpts from the English translation of the *Rite of Confirmation (Second Edition)* © 1975, ICEL. All rights reserved.

Come and, p. vi: Music can be found in *Songs and Prayers from Taizé,* GIA Publications, Inc., Chicago, 1991.

Outwardly, p. 2: *The Hours of the Divine Office in English and Latin,* Liturgical Press, Collegeville, 1964.

Lord, you, p. 2: *The Sacramentary,* Catholic Book Publishing Co., New York, 1985.

Lord God, p. 2; O God, p. 40; Then, letting, p. 50: *Early Christian Prayers,* Longmans, Green and Co. Ltd., London, 1961.

The soul faces, p. 4: *Gospel Light,* Crossroad Publishing Company, New York, © 1998. Used with permission.

Life in the spirit, p. 4: *The Roots of Christian Mysticism*, New City Press, Hyde Park, New York, 1995.

We worship, p. 5: *Your Word Is Near*, Newman Press, Westminster, Maryland, 1968.

Christ's friends, p. 7: *Hymns for Morning and Evening Prayer*, Liturgy Training Publications (LTP), Chicago, 1999. © Brother Aelred-Seton Shanley.

Lord, make me, p. 8; O Spirit, p. 14, Enter my, p. 20; O come, p. 36: *The Oxford Book of Prayer*, Oxford University Press, Oxford, 1985.

In the beginning, p. 9: *Revised Standard Version of the Bible* © 1952, Division of Christian Education of the National Council of Churches of Christ in the United States of America. All rights reserved.

God, the Spirit, p. 10: *Redeeming the Time*, GIA Publications, Inc., Chicago, 1997.

My spirit, p. 10: *The Hodder Book of Christian Prayers*, compiled by Tony Castle. Hodder and Stoughton Ltd., 1986.

You are, p. 11: *Catherine of Siena, The Dialogue*, translated by Suzanne Noffke, Paulist Press, Mahwah, New Jersey, 1980. Used with permission.

Christ was, p. 13; The Spirit, p. 16: *Drinking from the Hidden Fountain*, Cistercian Publications, Kalamazoo, Michigan, 1994.

All-powerful God, p. 17; It is from, p. 30; Lord Jesus, p. 33; The whole; The laying, p. 48; Father, we, p. 49; Be sealed, p. 50; Signed with, p. 51; God our, p. 52; Do you, pp. 54-55: from Rite of Confirmation in *The Rites of the Catholic Church*, Pueblo Publishing Co., New York, 1976.

Holy Mary, p. 20: *A Book of Prayers* © 1982, International Committee on English in the Liturgy (ICEL). All rights reserved?

Holy Spirit, pp. 22-23: Translated by Peter Scagnelli in *Paschal Mission 1995*, LTP.

Sing to, p. 24: *Revised Common Lectionary*.

Holy Breathing, p. 25: *It's Midnight, Lord*, translated by Joseph Gallagher. The Pastoral Press, Washington D.C., 1984.

May none, p. 27; O God, p. 28; Holy Spirit, p. 29; Grant me, p. 29; O God, p. 35; Dear God, p. 35; Thank you, p. 39; God be, p. 39; Christ has, p. 42; Give us, p. 43: *Eerdman's Book of Famous Prayers*, William B. Eerdmans Publishing Co., Grand Rapids, Michigan, 1984.

The scriptures, p. 31: Dogmatic Constitution on Divine Revelation in *Vatican Council II Constitutions, Decrees, Declarations*, edited by Austin Flannery, Costello Publishing Company, Northport, New York, 1996.

Every time, p. 34: Music can be found in *Lead Me, Guide Me*, GIA Publications, Inc., Chicago, 1997, no. 220.

It sounds, p. 37: *An Interrupted Life*. English translation © 1983 by Jonathan Cape Ltd. © 1981 by De Haan/Uniboek b.v., Bussum. Reprinted by permission of Pantheon Books, a division of Random House, Inc.

If baptism, p. 41: *Living Liturgy*, translated by Patricia A. Coulter and Julie Coulter-English, LTP, 1998.

God of tempest, p. 44: *Awake Our Hearts to Praise!* GIA Publications, Inc., Chicago, 2000.

Let us, p. 44: *Flames of the Spirit*, edited by Ruth C. Duck, The Pilgrim Press, New York, 1985.

Come, Holy Spirit, pp. 46–47 translated by Edward Caswall, 1849, alt., in *Sing Praise*, Franciscan Sisters of Perpetual Adoration, La Crosse, Wisconsin, 1992.

This holy, p. 49: quoted in *The Three Days*, LTP, 1992.

COME, HOLY SPIRIT!

LTP

LITURGY
TRAINING
PUBLICATIONS

ACKNOWLEDGMENTS

This book was compiled and edited by Lorie Simmons with assistance
from Margaret Brennan, Gabe Huck, David Philippart and Lorraine
Schmidt. Audrey Novak Riley was the production editor. Anne
Fritzinger designed the book and typeset it in Galliard. Printed by
Printing Arts Chicago. The art is by Vicki Shuck.

We are grateful to the many publishers and authors who have given
permission to include their work. Every effort has been made to
determine the ownership of all texts and to make proper arrangements
for their use. We will gladly correct in future editions any oversight or
error that is brought to our attention.

Resources cited on page 56.

COME, HOLY SPIRIT! © 2001 Archdiocese of Chicago: Liturgy Training
Publications, 1800 North Hermitage Avenue, Chicago IL 60622-1101;
1-800-933-1800; fax 1-800-933-7094; orders@ltp.org; www.ltp.org.
All rights reserved.

Library of Congress Control Number 2001087865.

05 04 03 02 01   5 4 3 2 1

ISBN 1-56854-284-4
PCONF

FOREWORD

The Holy Spirit pulses through us and through creation, but often we forget to notice. This book encourages noticing. The first section gives prayers for every day of the week to sharpen your spiritual senses. The second section is for specific times of joy or struggle—when praising, needing forgiveness, or seeking wisdom. A third section recalls confirmation. Go there to remember who you are and how you've been fortified to do God's work. Then revisit the baptismal promises at the end of the book.

Saint Paul says that the Spirit will help us pray: *for we do not know how to pray as we ought, but that very Spirit intercedes with sighs too deep for words* (Romans 8:26). Through these prayers and reflections, may you come to know the Holy Spirit who lives in us, teaches us and urges us to do service and justice.

COME AND PRAY IN·US, HOLY SPIRIT!

EVERY DAY WITH THE SPIRIT

Sunday

Come, Holy Spirit,
fill the hearts of your faithful;
and kindle in us the fire of your love.

When the time for Pentecost was fulfilled, they
were all in one place together. And suddenly
there came from the sky a noise like a strong
driving wind, and it filled the entire house in
which they were. Then there appeared to them
tongues as of fire, which parted and came to
rest on each one of them. And they were all
filled with the holy Spirit and began to speak in
different tongues, as the Spirit enabled them to
proclaim. . . . Peter proclaimed to them,
". . . God raised this Jesus: of this we are all
witnesses. Exalted at the right hand of God, he
received the promise of the holy Spirit from
the Father and poured it forth, as you both see
and hear."

—*Acts 2:1–4, 14a, 32–33, NAB*

Outwardly, tongues of fire appeared: inwardly,
their hearts were set ablaze; for when the
disciples received God under the appearance of
fire, they began to burn with a sweet love.

—*Saint Gregory, sixth century*

Lord, you are holy indeed,
the fountain of all holiness.
Let your Spirit come upon these gifts
    to make them holy,
so that they may become for us
the body and blood of our Lord, Jesus Christ.

—*from Eucharistic Prayer III of the Roman liturgy*

Lord God, you have made us fit
to have our sins forgiven
through the bath the Holy Spirit uses
to confer new birth.
By infusing your grace into us,
enable us to serve you as you will.

—*adapted from a prayer of Hippolytus, third century*

Monday

Come, Holy Spirit,
fill the hearts of your faithful;
and kindle in us the fire of your love.

The wind blows where it wills, and you can
hear the sound it makes, but you do not know
where it comes from or where it goes; so it is
with everyone who is born of the Spirit.

—_John 3:8, NAB_

The soul faces outward through the mind and body and into the world. Suddenly a door opens in the back of the soul, and Spirit enters. . . . In my imagination what is important is that it comes from the back. Spirit is not an object or person that can be seen. So it is not out in front to be observed, measured, described. I favor the sneak attack of a back door, suddenly opened by a combination of the soul's readiness and the Spirit's eagerness.

—*John Shea*

Life in the spirit means gradually becoming aware of "baptismal grace," and this awareness transforms the whole person.

—*Olivier Clément*

We worship you, Holy Spirit of God,
and we may only guess, as best we can,
who you are for us.
We call you by human names and words
so that we need not be entirely silent.
We open up our hearts to receive you
that we may learn how deeply
and invisibly you are present everywhere.
You are the air we breathe,
the distance we gaze into,
the space that surrounds us. . . .
We pray to you, Spirit of God, creator,
complete the work you have begun,
prevent the evil we are capable of doing
and inspire us toward what is good.

—*Huub Oosterhuis*

Tuesday

Come, Holy Spirit,
fill the hearts of your faithful;
and kindle in us the fire of your love.

The fruit of the Spirit is love, joy, peace,
patience, kindness, generosity, faithfulness,
gentleness, and self-control. If we live by the
Spirit, let us also be guided by the Spirit.

—*Galatians 5:22–23a, 25*

Christ's friends with Mary gather now,
united, one in heart and home;
in prayer they wait the promised gift,
receptive now to God's unknown.

The primal cosmic breath and fire
envelops them with searing pow'r:
creation's birth and Sinai's blaze
both consummated in this hour.

Each one God's holy temple now,
they speak of all they saw and heard;
with new-found tongues they now proclaim
what to the world will seem absurd.

Intoxicated by new wine,
still sober even as they reel,
their former sadness is displaced
by God's own joy, the Spirit's seal!

She forms new hearts and law within,
a new creation fashioning:
have we new eyes, new ways to see
her holiness in everything? Amen.

—*Aelred-Seton Shanley*

Lord, make me an instrument of your peace.
Where there is hatred, let me sow love;
where there is injury, pardon;
where there is doubt, faith;
where there is despair, hope;
where there is darkness, light;
where there is sadness, joy.

O divine Master,
Grant that I may not so much seek
to be consoled as to console,
to be understood as to understand.
to be loved as to love.

For it is in giving that we receive;
it is in pardoning that we are pardoned;
it is in dying that we are born to eternal life.

—*attributed to Saint Francis of Assisi, thirteenth century*

Wednesday

Come, Holy Spirit,
fill the hearts of your faithful;
and kindle in us the fire of your love.

In the beginning God created the heavens and
the earth. The earth was without form and
void, and darkness was upon the face of the
deep; and the Spirit of God was moving over
the face of the waters.

—*Genesis 1:1–2, RSV*

God, the Spirit, still creating,
flaming through the universe,
light, all suns and stars transcending,
come, the clouds of sin disperse!

Come to us who bow in wonder;
waken faith that will not die
till the hymn, "To God be glory!"
is the whole creation's cry!

—*Herman G. Stuempfle, Jr.*

My spirit is the Holy Spirit's.
Therefore I believe and confess my faith,
which is the source of light and life to me.
Blessed Father,
I, your creature,
would have you make me holy like yourself,
for you have given me
    every means to become so.
Glory is yours, now and always,
age after age. Amen.

—*anonymous, second century*

YOU·ARE A FIRE ALWAYS BURNING BUT·NEVER CONSUMING

CATHERINE OF SIENA

Thursday

Come, Holy Spirit,
fill the hearts of your faithful;
and kindle in us the fire of your love.

In those days Jesus came from Nazareth of
Galilee and was baptized by John in the
Jordan. And just as he was coming up out of
the water, he saw the heavens torn apart and
the Spirit descending like a dove on him. And a
voice came from heaven, "You are my son, the
Beloved; with you I am well pleased."

—*Mark 1:9–11*

Christ was anointed with spiritual oil, that is, with the Holy Spirit, called "oil of gladness." And you also have been anointed with ointment, chrism, so that you may be partakers with Christ, sharing his lot. This ointment, after the invocation, is no longer ordinary ointment: it is a gift from Christ which is able to confer on you the Holy Spirit.

While the body is being anointed with the visible oil, the soul is being consecrated with the holy and life-giving Spirit.

—*Cyril of Jerusalem, fourth century*

Our modern English word "chrism" comes from the Latin word "chrisma." Its root is the Greek verb "chriein," to anoint. Chrism is the consecrated oil used in baptism, confirmation and ordination.

Six days before the Passover Jesus came to Bethany, the home of Lazarus, whom he had raised from the dead. There they gave a dinner for him. Martha served, and Lazarus was one of those at the table with him. Mary took a pound of costly perfume made of pure nard, anointed Jesus' feet, and wiped them with her hair. The house was filled with the fragrance of the perfume.

—*John 12:1–3*

O Spirit of God, mighty river,
flow over me, in me, through me.
O Spirit of God, cleanse me,
purify the channels of my life.
O Spirit of God, bear me along,
with thy flood of life-giving service.
O Spirit of God, mighty fire,
glow in me, burn in me,
until thy radiance fills my soul.

—*Charles Devanesan*

Friday

Come, Holy Spirit,
fill the hearts of your faithful;
and kindle in us the fire of your love.

The spirit of the LORD shall rest
   on him,
the spirit of wisdom and understanding,
the spirit of counsel and might,
the spirit of knowledge
   and the fear of the LORD.

—_Isaiah 11:2_

When Jesus knew that all was now finished, he said (in order to fulfill the scripture), "I am thirsty." A jar full of sour wine was standing there. So they put a sponge full of the wine on a branch of hyssop and held it to his mouth. When Jesus had received the wine, he said, "It is finished." Then he bowed his head and gave up his spirit.

—*John 19:28–30*

The Spirit was present in the body of the Lord, his anointing and his inseparable companion. The church itself is the work of the Spirit.

—*Basil the Great, fourth century*

All-powerful God,
Father of our Lord Jesus Christ,
by water and the Holy Spirit
you free your sons and daughters from sin
and give them new life.
Send your Holy Spirit upon us
to be our Helper and Guide.
Give us the spirit of wisdom and understanding,
the spirit of right judgment and courage,
the spirit of knowledge and reverence.
Fill us with the spirit of wonder and awe
in your presence.
We ask this through Christ our Lord. Amen.

—adapted from the Rite of Confirmation, no. 25

Saturday

Come, Holy Spirit,
fill the hearts of your faithful;
and kindle in us the fire of your love.

The angel said to her. "The Holy Spirit will
come upon you, and the power of the Most
High will overshadow you; therefore the child
to be born will be holy; he will be called Son
of God."

—*Luke 1:35*

Holy Mary
Holy Mother of God
Mirror of justice
Throne of wisdom
Mystical rose
Tower of ivory
Ark of the covenant
Gate of heaven
Morning star

—*Litany of Loretto*

Enter my heart, O Holy Spirit,
come in blessed mercy and set me free.
Throw open, O Lord,
the locked doors of my mind.
O Holy Spirit, very God,
whose presence is liberty,
grant me the perfect freedom
to be thy servant
today, tomorrow, evermore.

—*Eric Milner-White*

VENI, SANCTE SPIRITUS

VENI, CREATOR SPIRITUS

Veni, Sancte Spiritus

Holy Spirit, Lord divine,
Come from heights of heav'n and shine,
  Come with blessed radiance bright!
Come, O Father of the poor,
Come, whose treasured gifts endure,
  Come, our heart's unfailing light!

Of consolers, wisest, best,
And our soul's most welcome guest,
  Sweet refreshment, sweet repose.
In our labor, rest most sweet,
Pleasant coolness in the heat,
  Consolation in our woes.

Light most blessed, shine with grace
In our heart's most secret place;
  Fill your faithful through and through!
Left without your presence here,
Life itself would disappear;
  Nothing thrives apart from you.

Cleanse our soiled hearts of sin,
Arid souls refresh within,
    Wounded lives to health restore.
Bend the stubborn heart and will,
Melt the frozen, warm the chill,
    Guide the wayward home once more.

On the faithful who are true
And profess their faith in you,
    In your sev'nfold gift, descend!
Give us virtue's sure reward,
Give us your salvation, Lord,
    Give us joys that never end!

—*Stephen Langton, twelfth century*

When the Spirit Moves Us

Beginning Something New

Sing to the LORD a new song,
the praise of God from the end of the earth!

> —*Isaiah 42:10, RCL*

I am about to do a new thing;
   now it springs forth,
   do you not perceive it?

> —*Isaiah 43:19*

I am about to create new heavens
   and a new earth;
the former things shall not be remembered
   or come to mind.

> —*Isaiah 65:17*

HOLY·BREATHING

OF·GOD, I·FEEL
YOU·STIRRING.
WARMED·BY
THIS·BREATH
GOOD·THINGS
GROW

DOM HELDER CAMARA

Praising and Thanking

How many are your works, O LORD!
In wisdom you have made them all.
The earth is full of your riches.

All of these look to you
to give them their food in due season.
You give it, they gather it up;
you open your hand, they have their fill.

You send forth your spirit, they are created;
and you renew the face of the earth.

I will sing to the LORD all my life,
make music to my God while I live.
May my thoughts be pleasing to God.
I find my joy in the LORD.

—Psalm 104:1, 24, 27–28, 30, 33–34

May none of God's wonderful works
    keep silence,
night or morning.
Bright stars, high mountains, the depths
    of the seas,
sources of rushing rivers:
may all these break into song
as we sing to Father, Son and Holy Spirit.
May all the angels in the heavens reply:
Amen! Amen! Amen!
Power, praise, honor, eternal glory
to God, the only Giver of grace.
Amen! Amen! Amen!

—*Egypt, third century*

O God, we thank you for this earth, our home;
for the wide sky and the blessed sun,
for the salt sea and the running water,
for the everlasting hills
and the never-resting winds,
for trees and the common grass underfoot.
We thank you for our senses
by which we hear the songs of birds,
and see the splendor of the summer fields,
and taste of the autumn fruits,
and rejoice in the feel of the snow,
and smell the breath of the spring.
Grant us a heart wide open to all this beauty;
and save our souls from being so blind
that we pass unseeing
when even the common thornbush
is aflame with your glory,
O God our creator,
who lives and reigns for ever and ever.

—*Walter Rauschenbusch*

Seeking Wisdom and Discernment

Holy Spirit
think through me
till your ideas
are my ideas.

   —*Amy Carmichael*

Grant me, O Lord,
to know what is worth knowing,
to love what is worth loving,
to praise what delights you most,
to value what is precious in your sight,
to hate what is offensive to you.
Do not let me judge by what I see,
nor pass sentence according to what I hear,
but to judge rightly between things that differ,
and above all to search out
and to do what pleases you,
through Jesus Christ our Lord.

   —*Thomas à Kempis, fourteenth century*

Jesus was speaking: "I have said these things to you while I am still with you. But the Advocate, the Holy Spirit, whom the Father will send in my name, will teach you everything, and remind you of all that I have said to you."

—*John 14:25–26*

It is from the hearing of the word of God that the many-sided power of the Holy Spirit flows upon the Church and upon each one of the baptized and confirmed, and it is by this word that God's will is manifest in the life of Christians.

—*Rite of Confirmation, no. 13*

The scriptures present God's own word in an unalterable form, and they make the voice of the holy Spirit sound again and again in the words of the prophets and apostles. . . . Such is the force and power of the word of God that it is the church's support and strength, imparting robustness to the faith of its daughters and sons and providing food for their souls. It is a pure and unfailing fount of spiritual life.

—*Second Vatican Council*

Needing Forgiveness

A new heart I will give you, and a new spirit I will put within you; and I will remove from your body the heart of stone and give you a heart of flesh. I will put my spirit within you, and make you follow my statutes and be careful to observe my ordinances. Then you shall live in the land that I gave to your ancestors; and you shall be my people, and I will be your God.

—*Ezekiel 36:26–28*

Have mercy on me, God, in your kindness.
In your compassion blot out my offense.

A pure heart create for me, O God,
put a steadfast spirit within me.
Do not cast me away from your presence,
nor deprive me of your holy spirit.

Give me again the joy of your help;
with a spirit of fervor sustain me,
that I may teach transgressors your ways
and sinners may return to you.

O rescue me, God, my helper,
and my tongue shall ring out your goodness.
O Lord, open my lips
and my mouth shall declare your praise.
For in sacrifice you take no delight,
burnt offering from me you would refuse;
my sacrifice, a contrite spirit,
a humbled, contrite heart you will not spurn.

—*Psalm 51:3, 12–16*

This short prayer has come to be known as the
Jesus Prayer and is often repeated over and over:

Lord Jesus Christ, Son of God,
have mercy on me, a sinner!

—*Rite of Penance, no. 92*

Weathering the Storms Within

O God, grant us the serenity
to accept what cannot be changed,
the courage to change what can be changed,
and the wisdom to know the difference.

—*Reinhold Niebuhr*

Dear God, make me think about what
    I'm doing
with my mind
with my body
with my habits
with my study
with my friends
with my hopes
with my parents
with my faith
with life.

—*Carl Burke*

O come, Holy Spirit,
inflame my heart,
set it on fire with love.
Burn away my self-centeredness
so that I can love unselfishly.
Breathe your life-giving breath
into my soul
so that I can live freely and joyously,
unrestricted by self-consciousness,
and may be ready to go
wherever you may send me.
Come like a gentle breeze
and give me your still peace
so that I may be quiet
and know the wonder of your presence.
Never leave me,
O Lord and giver of life!

—*Michael Hollings and Etta Gullick*

Facing Death

If the Spirit of the one who raised Jesus from the dead dwells in you, the one who raised Christ from the dead will give life to your mortal bodies also through his Spirit that dwells in you.

—*Romans 8:11, NAB*

It sounds paradoxical: By excluding death from our life we cannot live a full life, and by admitting death into our life we enlarge and enrich it. This has been my first real confrontation with death. I never knew what to make of it before. I have never seen a dead person. Just imagine: A world sown with a million corpses, and in twenty-seven years I have never seen a single one. I never delved deeply into the question: there was no need for that. And now death has come as large as life and part of it.

—*Etty Hillesum*

LORD, you have probed me, you know me:
    you know when I sit and stand;
    you understand my thoughts from afar.
My travels and my rest you mark;
    with all my ways you are familiar.
Even before a word is on my tongue,
    LORD, you know it all.

You formed my inmost being;
    you knit me in my mother's womb.
I praise you, so wonderfully you made me;
    wonderful are your works!
Your eyes foresaw my actions;
    in your book all are written down;
    my days were shaped,
        before one came to be.

How precious to me are your designs, O God;
    how vast the sum of them!

—Psalm 139:1–4, 13–14, 16–17, NAB

Seeking Strength and Protection

Thank you, Lord Jesus,
that you will be our hiding place,
whatever happens.

—*Corrie ten Boom*

God be in my head
and in my understanding;
God be in my eyes
and in my looking;
God be in my mouth
and in my speaking;
God be in my heart
and in my thinking;
God be at my end
and at my departing.

—*from an English prayer book, sixteenth century*

O God of the powers,
Helper of every soul that turns to you,
and turning,
finds itself under the strong hand
    of the Only Son:
we beg you through your divine power,
the power we cannot see,
the power of our Lord and Savior Jesus Christ,
that we, confirmed by the seal
    of the Holy Spirit,
may remain steadfast and immovable,
safe and free from harm.
May no one ill-treat us or conspire against us.
May we believe and know the truth
    all our lives long;
may we live in hope of receiving the life
    of heaven
and ever await the eternity promised us
by our Lord and Savior, Jesus Christ.
Through him may glory and power be yours,
now and age after age. Amen.

   —*adapted from the prayer book of Serapion,*
    fourth century

Reflecting on Service

If baptism produces an internal illumination,
confirmation changes it into a beacon's light.
If baptism lights a lamp within us, with
confirmation this lamp is lifted up onto a
lampstool, that is, put to the benefit of the
community. If baptism is something the
faithful come to enjoy in a rather passive
manner, confirmation arms us for battle. . . .
Confirmed Christians must not keep the light
closed in within themselves; rather, it is to be
placed at the service of others.

—*Sofia Cavalletti*

Now there are varieties of gifts, but the same
Spirit; and there are varieties of services, but
the same Lord; and there are varieties of
activities, but it is the same God who activates
all of them in everyone. To each is given the
manifestation of the Spirit for the common
good. All these are activated by one and the
same Spirit, who allots to each one individually

just as the Spirit chooses. For just as the body is one and has many members, and all the members of the body, though many, are one body, so it is with Christ. For in the one Spirit we were all baptized into one body—Jews or Greeks, slaves or free—and we were all made to drink of one Spirit.

—*1 Corinthians 12:4–7, 11–13*

Christ has no body now on earth but yours;
yours are the only hands with which he can do
    his work,
yours are the only feet with which he can go
    about the world,
yours are the only eyes through which
    his compassion
can shine forth upon a troubled world.
Christ has no body now on earth but yours.

—*Teresa of Avila, sixteenth century*

Finding Confidence for Discipleship

Jesus said, "John baptized with water, but you will be baptized with the Holy Spirit not many days from now. You will receive power when the Holy Spirit has come upon you; and you will be my witnesses in Jerusalem, in all Judea and Samaria, and to the ends of the earth."

—_Acts 1:5, 8_

Give us courage, O Lord, to stand up
    and be counted,
to stand up for those who cannot stand up
    for themselves,
to stand up for ourselves when it is needful
    for us to do so.

—_Alan Paton_

God of tempest, God of whirlwind,
as on Pentecost descend!
Drive us out from sheltered comfort!
Past these walls your people send!
Sweep us into costly service
there with Christ to bear the cross,
there with Christ to bear the cross!

God of passion, God unsleeping,
stir in us love's restlessness!
Where the people cry in anguish,
may we share your heart's distress.
Rouse us from content with evil;
claim us for your kingdom's work,
claim us for your kingdom's work!

—*Herman G. Stuempfle, Jr.*

Let us go now as spirited people, powerful as
the wind in doing God's will, energetic as fire
in extending the love of Christ. Be builders of
understanding and makers of peace.

—*Glen E. Rainsley*

LORD, SEND·OUT YOUR SPIRIT, AND·RENEW THE·FACE OF·THE EARTH

PSALM 104:30

Veni, Creator Spiritus

Come, Holy Spirit, by whose breath
Life rises vibrant out of death:
Come to create, renew, inspire;
Come, kindle in our hearts your fire.

You are the seeker's sure resource,
Of burning love the living source,
Protector in the midst of strife,
The giver and the Lord of life.

In you God's energy is shown,
To us your varied gifts made known.
Teach us to speak; teach us to hear;
Yours is the tongue and yours the ear.

Flood our dull senses with your light;
In mutual love our hearts unite.
Your pow'r the whole creation fills;
Confirm our weak uncertain wills.

From inner strife grant us release;
Turn nations to the ways of peace;
To fuller life your people bring,
That as one body we may sing.

Through you may we the Creator learn
And know the Son and you discern;
You come from both, and we'll adore
In perfect faith forevermore.

—*Rabanus Maurus, ninth century*

CONFIRMATION

The Confirming Community Calls the Spirit

The whole people of God, represented by the families and friends of the candidates and by members of the local community, will be invited to take part in the celebration and will express its faith in the fruits of the Holy Spirit.

—*Rite of Confirmation, no. 4*

The laying of hands on the candidates by the bishop and the concelebrating priests is the biblical gesture by which the gift of the Holy Spirit is invoked.

—*Rite of Confirmation, no. 9*

When we call out "Come, Holy Spirit!" we are invoking the Spirit. The word "invoke" comes from the Latin "vocare," meaning "to call." We also invoke the Spirit when we make an earnest request, or when, by our fervent trust, we put the Spirit into effect in our lives.

The Chrism and the Anointing

This holy chrism, a mixture of olive oil and perfume will be used to anoint infants after baptism, those who are to be confirmed, bishops and priests at their ordination and altars and churches at the time of their dedication.

—*U.S. Bishops' Committee on the Liturgy*

Father, we ask you to bless this oil
you have created.
Fill it with the power of your Holy Spirit
through Christ your Son.
Make this chrism a sign of life and salvation
for those who are to be born again in
    the waters of baptism.
Grant them royal, priestly and prophetic honor,
and clothe them with incorruption.
May they come to share eternal life
in the glory of your kingdom.

—*Consecration of Chrism*

In the fourth century, the bishop anointed the newly baptized in this way:

Then, letting the blessed oil run from his hand and applying it to the head of the newly baptized, he says: "I anoint you with holy oil in the name of the Lord—the almighty Father, Jesus Christ and the Holy Spirit." After the anointing, he kisses them, saying: "The Lord be with you." The baptized reply: "May he be with your spirit too."

—Hippolytus, fourth century

Be sealed with the Gift of the Holy Spirit.

R. Amen.

—Rite of Confirmation, no. 27

Signed with the perfumed oil, the baptized person receives the indelible character, the seal of the Lord, together with the gift of the Spirit.

—*Rite of Confirmation*

Our word "seal" comes from the Latin word "sigilium," related to the Latin word "signum," that is, "sign." So a seal is a sign that confirms, ratifies or makes secure. Important legal documents often bear a seal to show that they are authentic and official. Before modern times, these seals were often bits of wax with a pattern pressed into them—the insignia of the authority behind the document. The impression might come from a raised or engraved pattern on a signet ring or something similar. This suggests that, in one sense, the Spirit impresses its divine pattern into our softened hearts, showing whose we are.

Going Forth

God our Father
made us his children by water and
   the Holy Spirit:
may God bless us
and watch over us with fatherly love.

Jesus Christ the Son of God
promised that the Spirit of truth
would be with his church for ever:
may he bless us and give us courage
in professing the true faith.

The Holy Spirit
came down upon the disciples
and set their hearts on fire with love:
may he bless us,
keep us one in faith and love
and bring us to the joy of God's kingdom.

May almighty God bless us,
the Father, and the Son, + and the Holy Spirit.

—adapted from the Rite of Confirmation, no. 33

THE·SPIRIT
OF·THE·LORD
GOD·IS·UPON
ME, BECAUSE
THE·LORD·HAS
ANOINTED·ME

ISAIAH 61:1

THE FAITH WE PROFESS

Do you reject Satan and all his works
and all his empty promises?

Do you believe in God the Father almighty,
creator of heaven and earth?

Do you believe in Jesus Christ,
his only Son, our Lord,
who was born of the Virgin Mary,
was crucified, died, and was buried,
rose from the dead, and is now seated
at the right hand of the Father?

Do you believe in the Holy Spirit,
the Lord, the giver of life,
who came upon the apostles at Pentecost
and today is given to you sacramentally
   in confirmation?